ORIGINS

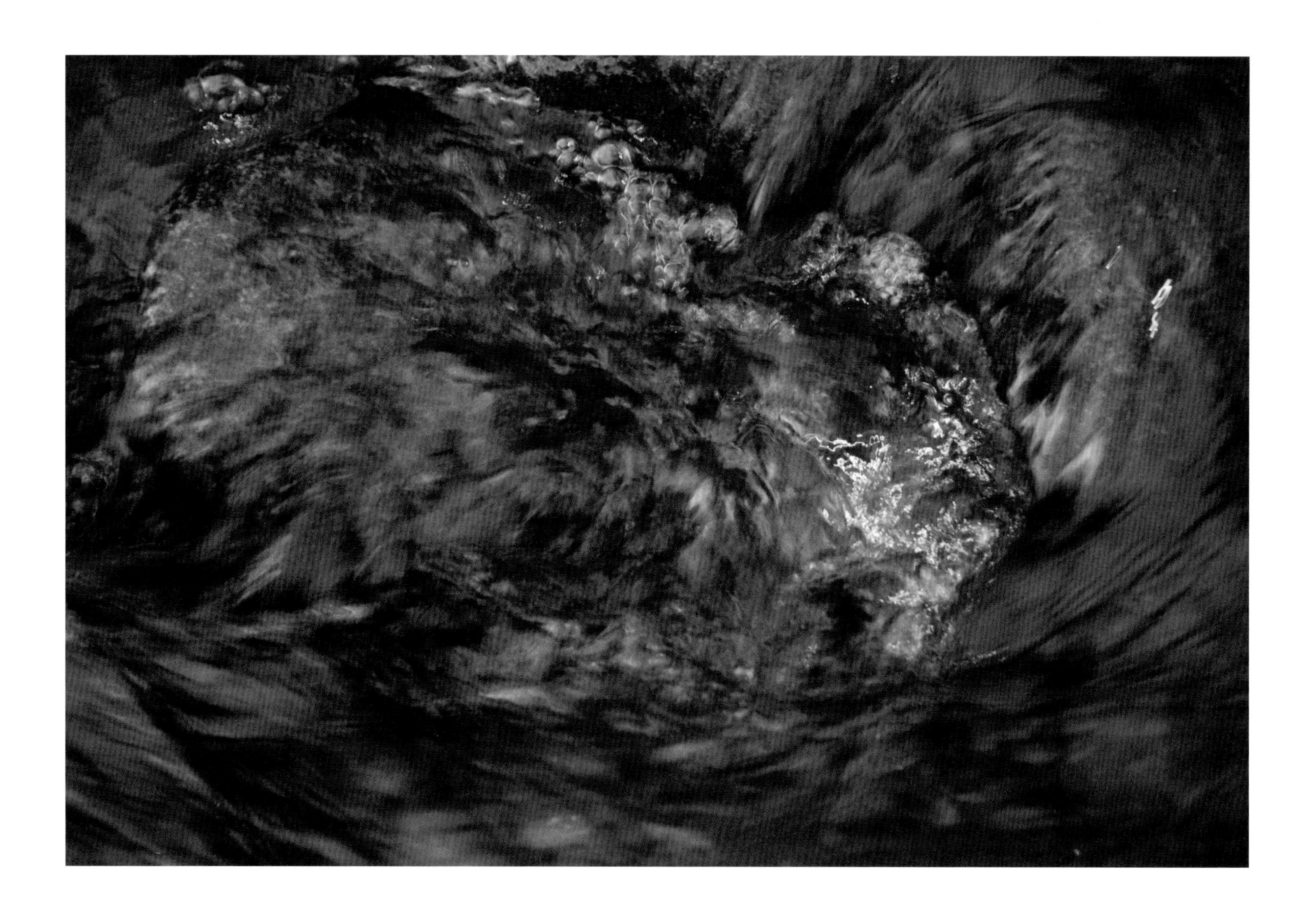

Jennifer Gough-Cooper

ORIGINS

song of Nooitgedacht
a remote valley in the Karoo

Jennifer Gough-Cooper
2011

"To see a World in a Grain of Sand
And a Heaven in a Wild Flower,
Hold Infinity in the palm of your hand
And Eternity in an hour."

William Blake

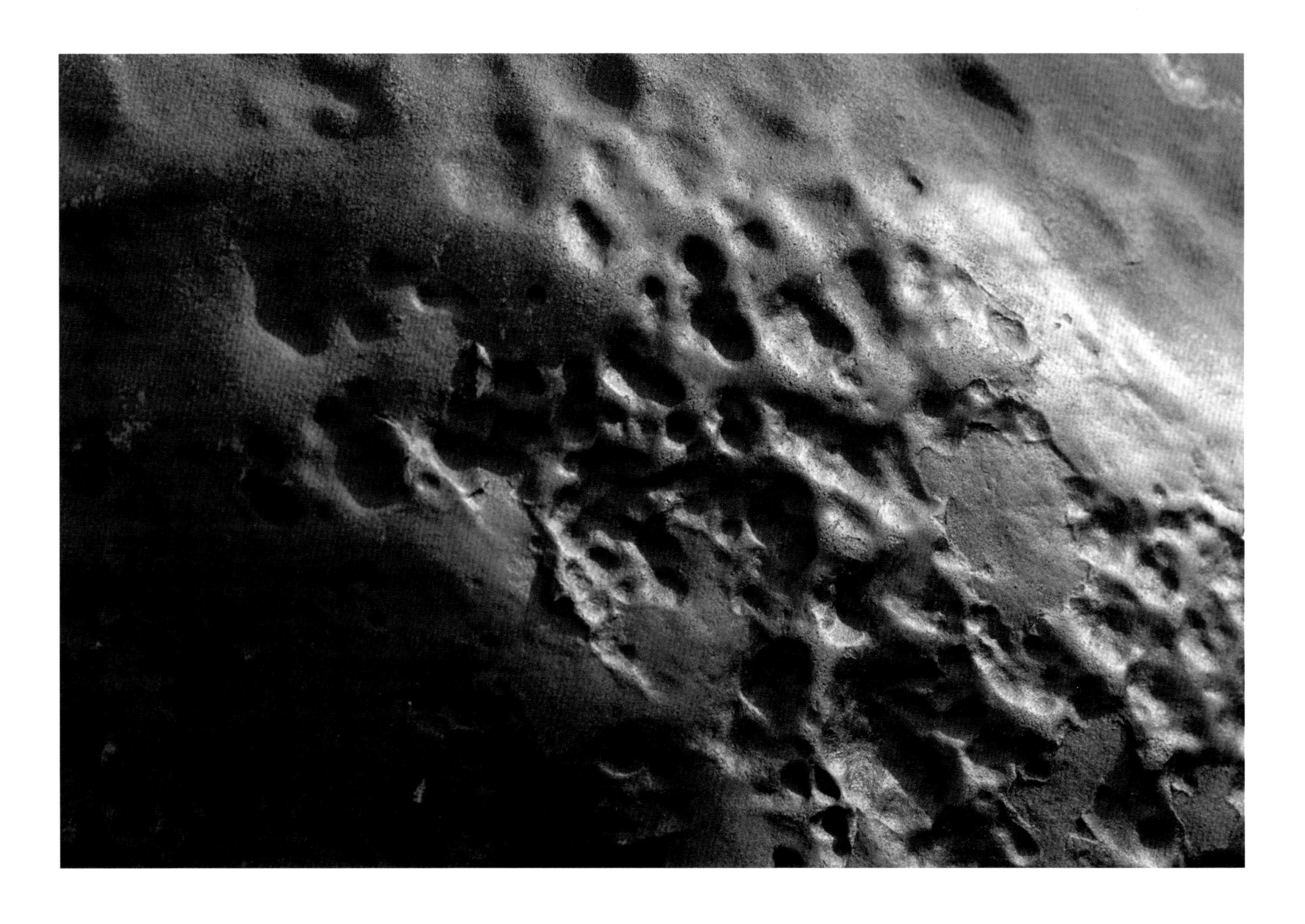

Beginnings

a song without words molten earth

chase of particles emerging light lifts the land

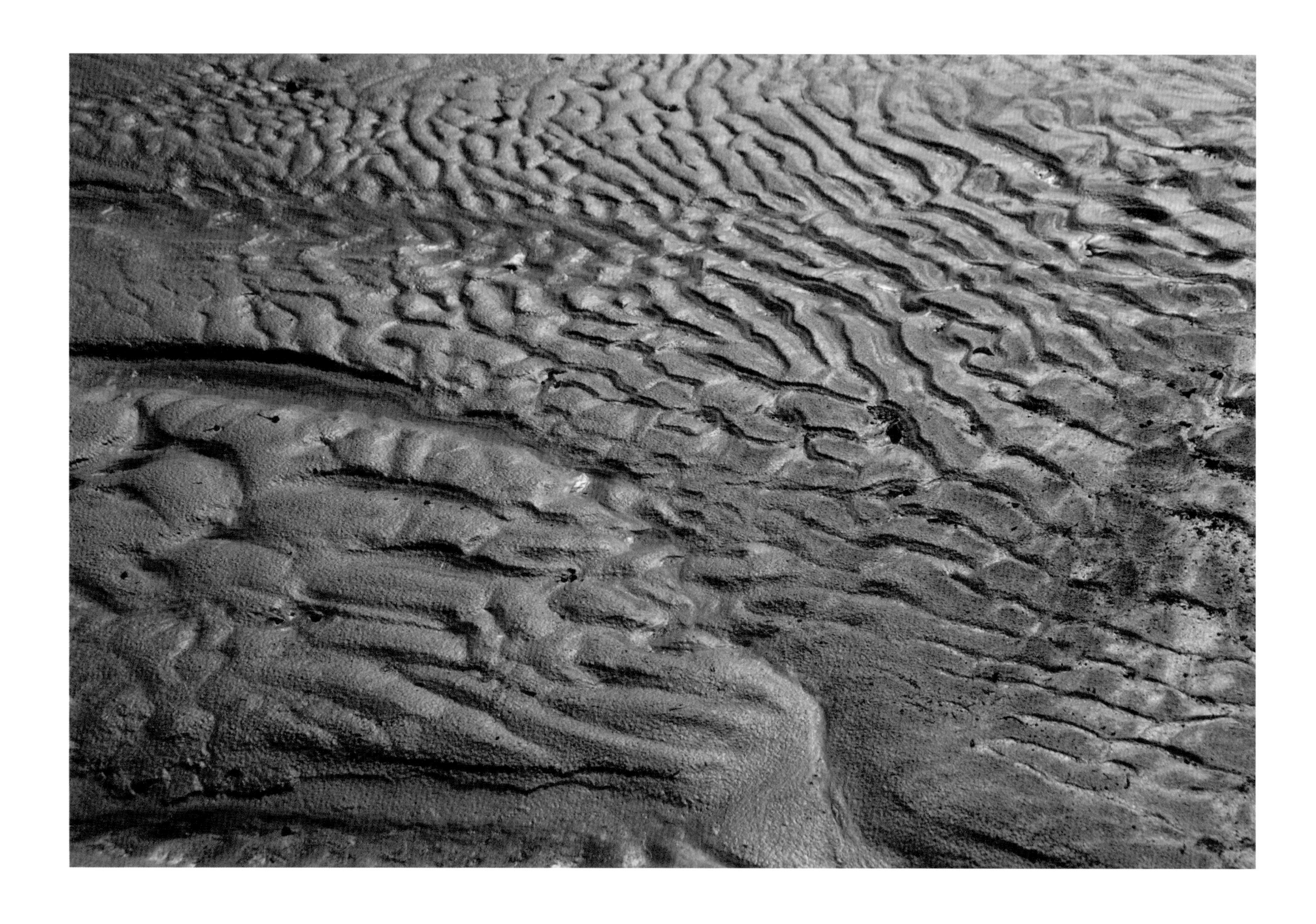

spectrum

Genesis by fire

turbulence of creation

echoes of infinity

making of mountains and valley

tumultuous waters

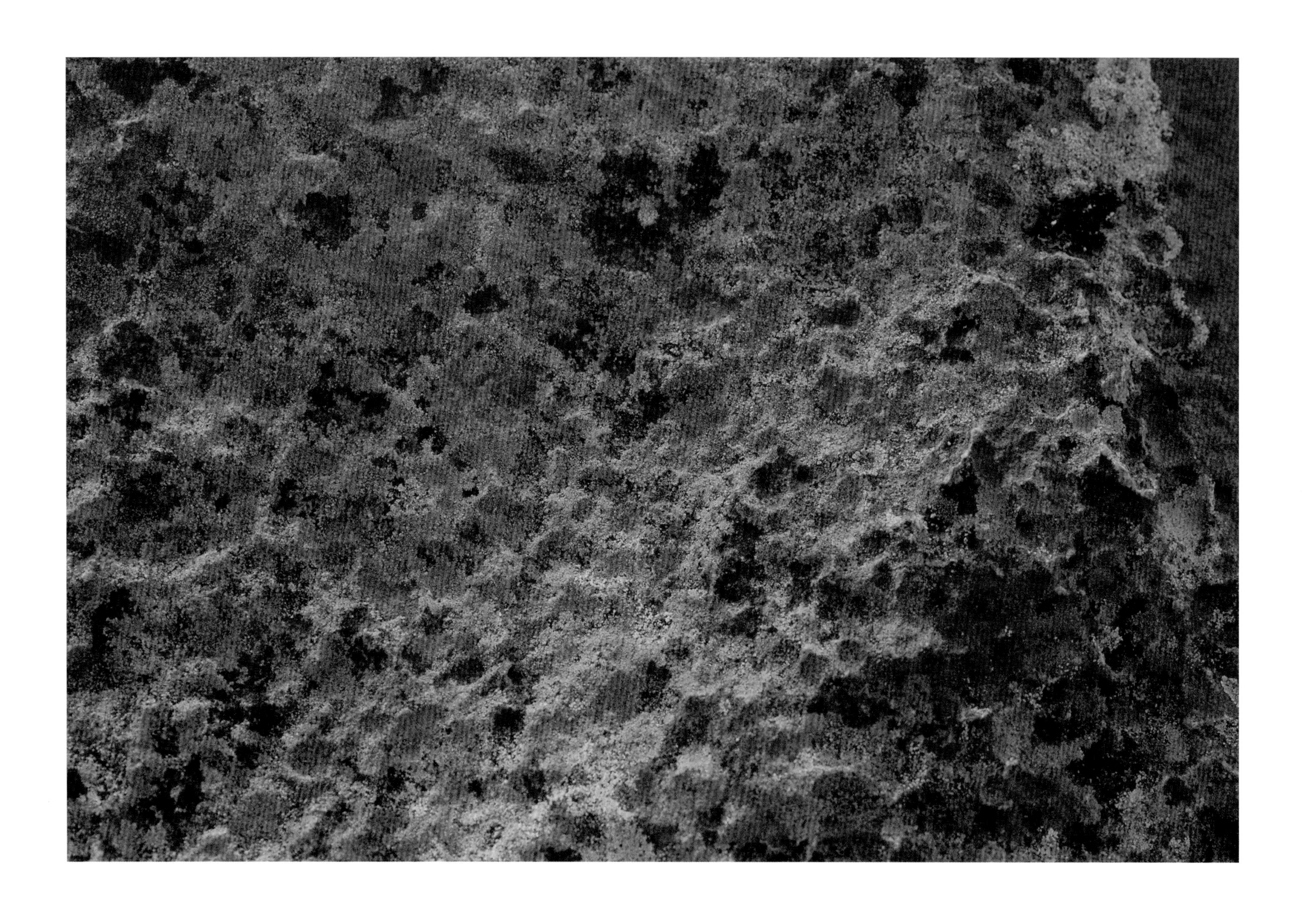

Here there had been an ancient sea

progression of lake into marsh from silt to shale: reconstitution

slow whittled patterning of the earth: erosion

The story is written in stone

great chronologies layered in the earth moving in ancient time

abrupt storms interrupt paths erased, anonymity

Passage of Man

a story already walked through breathe the light

gaze into vista the circle of gifts enters the cycle of nature

Realm without maps

floral kingdoms to east and west   permanence and mutability

appearances and disappearances   like rumours through history

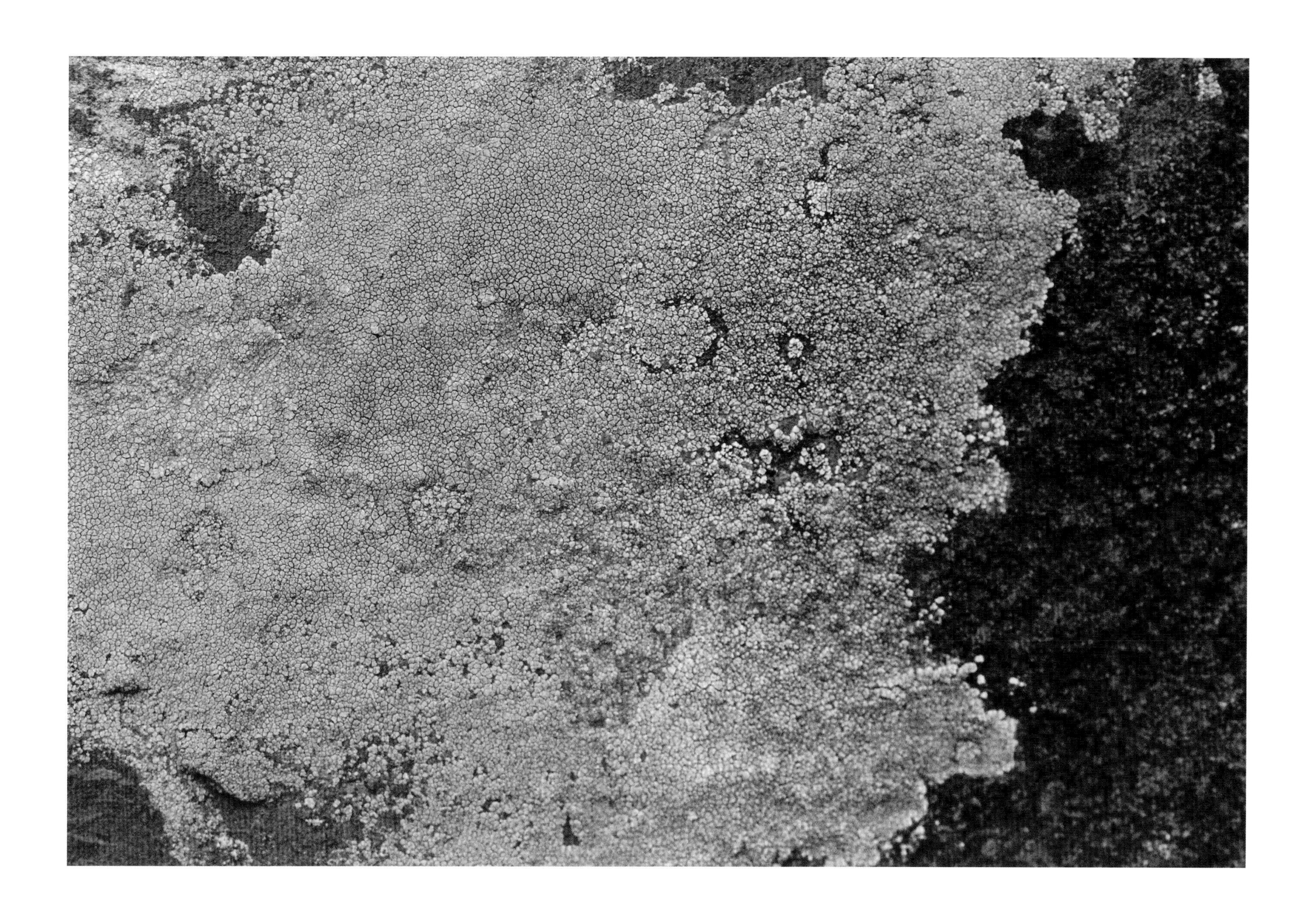

incident

Find beauty be still

Earth is small, blue and alone

energies   orders and rhythms   draw with light, make visible

time to stare

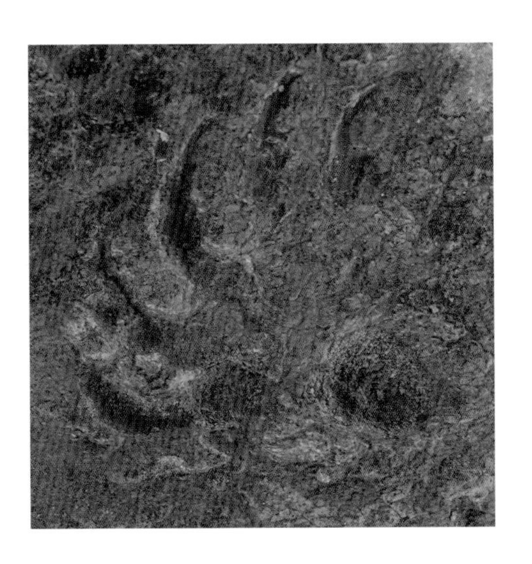

Dark shadow of the valley

turning of bone and leaf into eternity dispersing along paths

mounds and shards reflection

cause for wonder

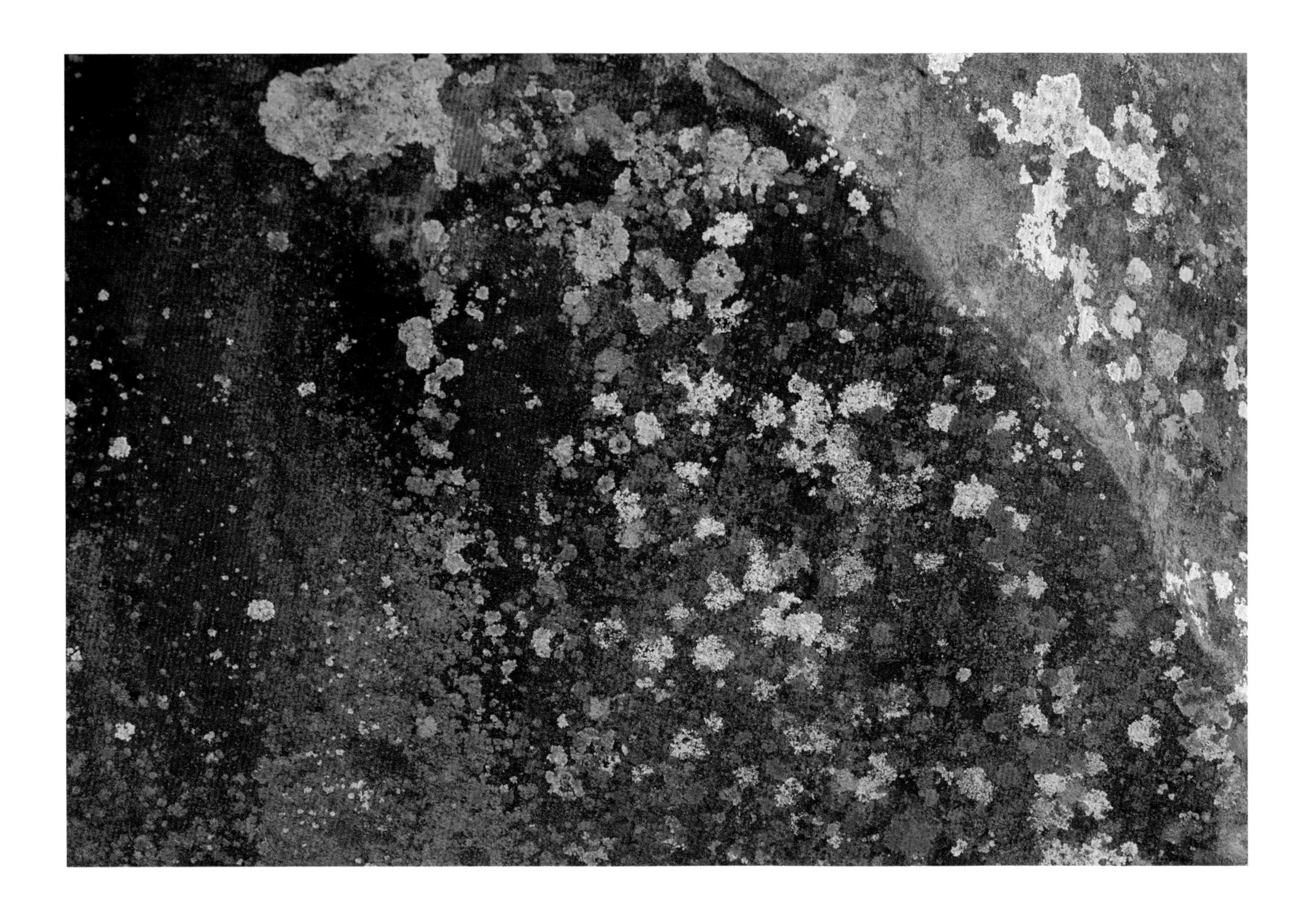

Returning red

reflecting redness galaxies at hand and far beyond

compass of the sun

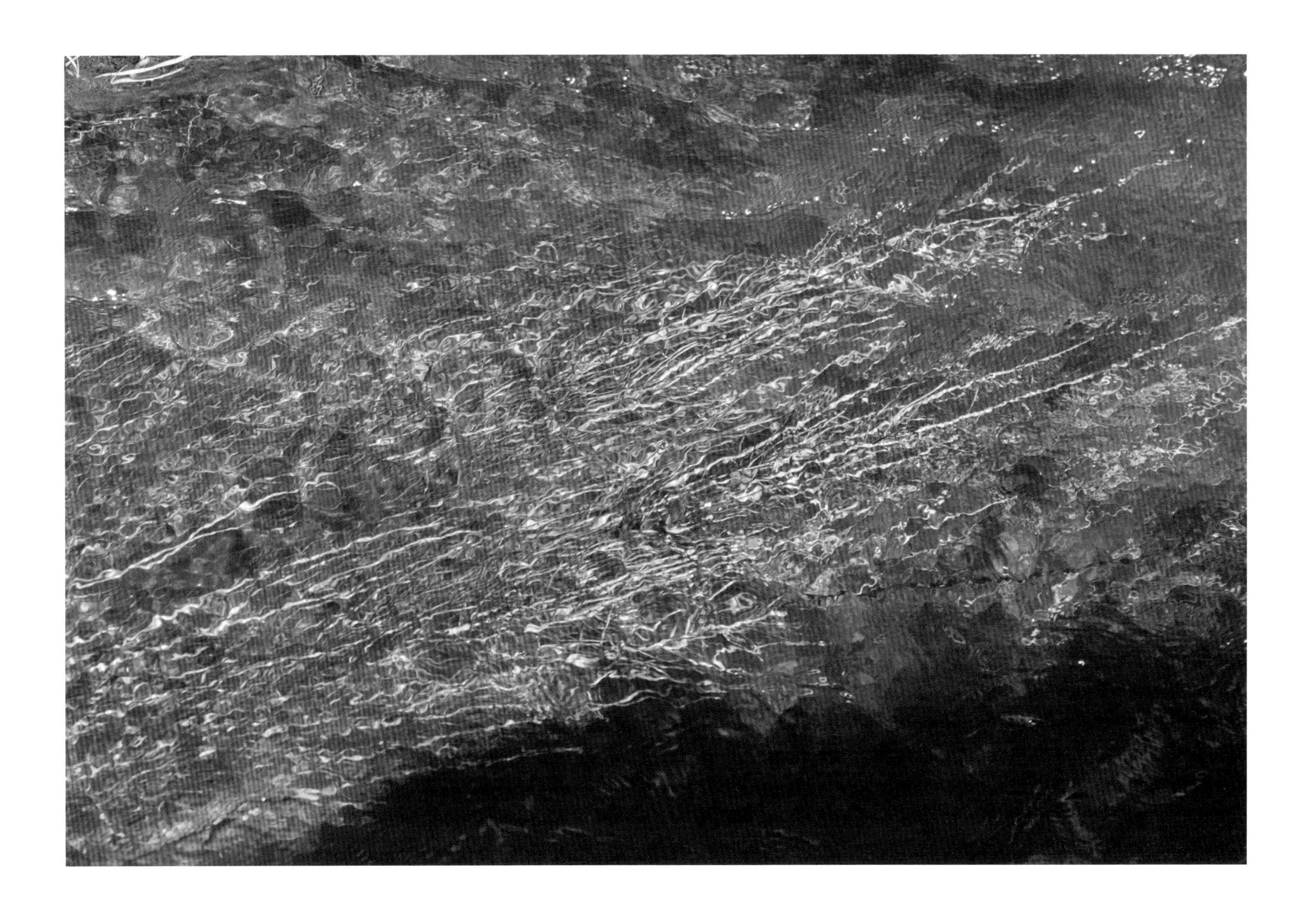

orientation

Groot-Suurkop
(2003m)
Rooiberge
Eselkop
(1552m)

Skurwekop
(1792m)

Bakenskop

Tolkop

Siaskop
(1794m)

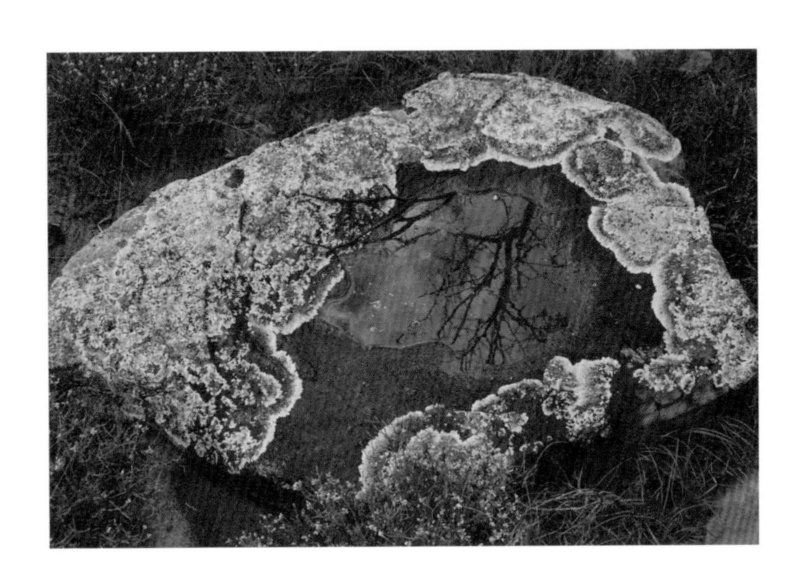

NOTES ON THE PHOTOGRAPHS

On my first visit to Nooitgedacht[1] in 2002, I found a place of serenity, the surrounding mountains protective of the plain. There is a distinct air of timelessness in the landscape. This ancient valley, I discovered, has evolved over millions of years since its creation at the time of Gondwana.

I found inspiration for the form of the book only later in my exploration of the valley. One day, certain individual rocks in the landscape caught my attention: the surface of one huge boulder resembled our planet as one might imagine it in its molten state, straight from the fire of creation; another was scribbled with lines by a mysterious wayward writer; yet another was host to such an incredible pattern of fiery lichen, it appeared like a painting of galaxies travelling in infinite space. Clearly, the valley was characterised by its rock, the ancient bones of the earth.

To define this place, Fire, Air, Rock and Water are recurrent themes: Fire, in terms of sunlight and lichen; Air, described by atmosphere and morning mist; Rock, in which the valley's history is embedded; and, not least, Water, the precious and essential source of life and of survival itself. Water, with its visual extremes of mood and movement, its correspondences with Rock, its reflective qualities and its strength with wind to erode, has seeped steadily into these pages.

The photographs are presented in the spirit of a song – a melodic line – evoking these natural treasures in tempo with the slow cycles of infinite time at Nooitgedacht: a place, as its name suggests, truly beyond imagination.

Frontispiece — Vortex: Water's turbulent force.

Page 6 — A large meteorite-like boulder symbolizes beginnings: a projectile shooting through darkness amongst fiery bodies in the vast space of the Universe. This world within a world has a rock crust of manganese oxide, or pyrolusite. Resting like a way-marker on the broad dolerite sill of a hillside, it has long been used as a rubbing stone by large mammals.

[1] Nooitgedacht is located east of Graaff-Reinet in the Eastern Cape Province of South Africa. This Afrikaans word translates loosely to mean "not conceived of" or, "beyond imagination".

Pages 8 & 9	The strengthening light of the rising sun burns its way through thick mist, a miraculous combination of essential life-giving elements.
Pages 10 &11	A dolerite rock hosts encroaching lichen, one of the most ancient forms of life. Against the persistent endeavours of wind and water, the pock-marked rock surface displays differential weathering: the content of certain crystals in certain areas of the rock are more resistant to weathering. / Water has filtered down steep slopes after rain; combining forces, it courses over rocks creating a fizzing, hydrating flow.
Pages 12 & 13	After a passage of flash-flooding, the sculpted mud, fashioned by the fast-flowing current, starts drying in the sun. / Lying in the river, a jointed sandstone bedrock has been worn smooth by the insistent, abrasive action of water pouring over it.

spectrum

Page 15	A ray of sun catching a passing shower produces a fleeting rainbow: pure colour of light.

Genesis by fire [red]

Page 16	Like an apparition of the rising sun, grey lichen colonises the sharp edge of a blood-red sandstone rock.
Pages 18 & 19	Orange lichen liberally coats the ridges and dimples of a dolerite boulder. Within the dolerite, nodules of feldspar crystals resist the process of weathering creating a miniature landscape of hills, vales and craters.
Pages 20 & 21	A shallow stream, with dappled deep-red bed, transports fallen leaves. / Wedged red amongst pebbles in clear mountain waters, rests a small baked sandstone rock.
Page 22	Reminder of its amphibian ancestors so abundant in Permian and Triassic times, the frog crouches motionless in the river.

Here there had been an ancient sea [silver brown]

Page 24

Resembling planet Earth from outer space, a glassy sandstone boulder demonstrating onion-skin weathering, is host to continents of silvery-edged lichen.

Pages 26 & 27

Loose, unconsolidated material lies on the bed of a dry river course which, freshly redrawn after rain, resembles a braided river system with sand bar. / At high altitude, silver-grey segmented lichen snakes its way across rock.

Pages 28 & 29

After thunder and heavy rain, a dry river bed is transformed within an hour to a raging flood, carrying in its torrent silt and debris.

Pages 30 & 31

On the plain, a platform of white sandstone slabs stands at the edge of the river; in front of and behind this striking rock formation lie areas of dark gravel sculpted by swift water.

Pages 32 & 33

Flower-like forms rise from lichen. / A trackway formed some 250 million years ago by a dicynodont called Aulacephalodon on a patch of muddy inland seashore at the time of Gondwana, is revealed momentarily by steady erosion. An evolutionary link between reptile and mammal, these creatures inhabited this place well before the Dinosaurs. Over millions of years, volcanic eruptions and significant land movements built up layers of deposits burying the perfectly preserved trackway to the depth of a kilometre or more. Then slowly, steadily, the rock eroded over time, until one day these fossilized tracks miraculously reappeared on the plain. Now nothing prevents the friable rock of the tracks from crumbling into dust. The cycle continues.

Pages 34 & 35

A breeze ripples the surface of a swift-flowing river. / A fossilized surface of asymmetrical paleo-ripples carrying sediment, is studded with small bi-valves from the shore of the inland sea as it was 250 million years ago.

Page 36

A freshwater crab, its Crustacean ancestors dating from the Mesozoic era, negotiates the shallows of the river.

The story is written in stone [ochre]

Page 38

On the shelf of a dry river bed, a section of silt stone is patterned with yellow (iron-oxide) and brown (manganese oxides), caused by ground water trickling down a vertical fissure in the rock, which has later split, exposing its cryptic, scribbled face:a mysterious tablet of signs.

Pages 40 & 41

The cliff face of a dry river course constructed by successive pulses of sediment flood-events is built with a layer of red-brown mudstone, followed by zigzag layers of shale, with thicker silt stone above that. / In another area of the same ravine, successive pulses of flood events have resulted in the deposits of finer layers of mud, now converted into shale.

Pages 42 & 43

The mountain known today as Skurwekop, rises to 1,792 metres and dominates the southern horizon of the valley. Its 'skewed' summit of dolerite, or exceptionally hard iron stone, was created by intrusion of magma into the sediment pile some 190 million years ago during the period marking great upheaval and the breaking up of Gondwana. The horizontal sills on the flanks of the mountain are the result of a later period of magma injecting itself into the horizontal sediments, laid down by ancient rivers 250 million years ago. The softer sedimentary rock erodes more easily, leaving the hard magma sills to emphasise the contours of the present land-scape, so characteristic of the Karoo in Southern Africa. / On the plain beneath Skurwekop, a few Zebra and Ostrich graze with a big herd of Eland.

Pages 44 & 45

Seed-scattering grasses and vegetation on the plain are dried and dormant.

Pages 46 & 47

In addition to Earth, Air, Fire, and Water, Wood: the muscular trunk of a mature Pepper tree, *Schinus molle*, which was introduced to Africa from South America. With its graphic patterns, the grain in the heart of a fallen tree echoes movement in water and wind.

Pages 48 & 49

Percussion marks, or shatter cone patterns, caused by a sudden fracture of the rock, resemble certain reflections and ripples in shallow water gliding over smooth rock.

Page 50

A descendant of the Anapsida, the most primitive of reptiles that flourished in Permo-Triassic times, the tortoise swims in the still water of a dam.

Passage of Man [gold]

Page 52

Clearly defined lapping and swirling patterns of water appear on the smallest of scales as the stream flows through rocks.

Pages 54 & 55

A veritable mosaic of ripples, as shallow water runs across golden gravel, and a water-weathered sandstone boulder almost pulsates with colour lying in a dark corner of the river bed.

Pages 56 & 57

Elevated views sweep south across the valley to Skurwekop, / and to Siaskop in the west.

Pages 58 & 59

The reflection of a golden sunset is caught in tiny bubbles on the water's surface of a dam overflowing onto grassland. / A knobbly boulder is sprinkled with lichen as exquisite as gold-leaf.

Page 60

The fading image of a hunter-gatherer in full chase symbolizes the appearance about 2.5 million years ago of Man: a newcomer to the ancient planet. This tiny painting adorns the underside of a massive sandstone boulder standing in a cleft of the mountains amongst other high rocky vantage points.

Realm without maps [yellow]

Page 62

A vibrant patch of *Helichrysum subglomeratum* inhabits a sheltered corner of Suurkloof: a steep, curving valley, rich in flora, which descends from the summit of the Sneeuberg, part of the Great Escarpment of Southern Africa.

Pages 64 & 65

One bright, still morning, a herd of Lechwe grazes on the plain near a reservoir, known as Petersburg Dam. This dam is situated close to the old village of Petersburg, reduced to a few scattered bricks with only its church and school surviving, and the nearby farmstead of Nooitgedacht, built by Dutch settlers in 1819.

Pages 66 & 67

From a slope, high up Suurkloof, the view extends south across and beyond the valley to Eselkop (1,552m). The steep slopes of Suurkloof are host to a very rich mix of afromontane species including grey pools of *Helichrysum splendidum* and shrubs of *Euryops galpinii*, one of five species of *Euryops* in this valley. Here, the Daisy family (Asteraceae) is particularly well represented./ *Euryops galpinii* also appears in the foreground of the view due west from the Rooiberg ooking across and beyond the valley to the pyramidal-shaped mountain known as Siaskop (1,794 m).

Pages 68 & 69

Colonies of deep yellow and lemon lichen spread across sandstone.

Page 70

Leaves of the familiar *Acacia karroo*, or Sweet thorn, unfurl. / A bud of *Euryops proteoides*, a completely new species, when open, reveals a yellow daisy-type flower. It's a most remarkable marriage of *Euryops* with *Protea*. One of two new species of *Euryops* here (the other is *Euryops exsudans*), it grows in a colony of large Protea-like bushes at high altitude under the shelter of a cliff on the Sneeuberg overlooking Suurkloof.

Situated midway between the floral kingdom of the Cape in the west, and the kingdom of the Drakensberg in the east, on the summits here and in Suurkloof, fynbos plants and other species characteristic of the Cape mingle with treasures of the Drakensberg.

incident

Page 73

Threatening weather hangs over Waterkloof after an overnight fall of snow.

Find beauty: be still [emerald green]

Page 74

A winter sun gradually emerges over the valley.

Pages 76 & 77

Shadows shorten as the sun rises above the Rooiberg. / A resistant dolerite sill provides a natural, broad ledge used in a section of track climbing Suurkloof, a route built more than two centuries ago by the intrepid Voortrekkers for their journey through the valley, taking their ox-wagons across the mountains to Cradock and beyond.

Pages 78 & 79 The flat summit of the Rooiberg provides ample grazing above Glenhaven; the horizon to the north is dominated by the twin peaks of Nardousberg, rising to 2,326 and 2,429m, the latter being the second highest mountain in the Sneeuberg.

Pages 80 & 81 Water from Glenhaven spills through boulders of hornfels, a metamorphic sediment baked by the extreme heat of dolerite intrusion. / Long strands of weed stream out in the lower reaches of the Melk river which rises in this valley.

Pages 82 & 83 New stems of *Blechnum australe* subsp. *australe* reach out from a cranny in Suurkloof. / Old olive trees, *Olea europaea* subsp. *Africana*, stand near the river at the foot of Waterkloof.

Page 84 A Gemsbok leaps across the Melk river.

Earth is small, blue and alone [blue]

Page 86 The familiar shape of Skurwekop looms out of the morning mist.

Pages 88 & 89 Mist swirls in the valley; the sun gradually evaporates the mist lingering in the hollows between a series of ridges ranging towards the Rooiberg in the east.

Pages 90 & 91 Layers of mud transformed into shale lie in the wall of a dry river canyon; a detail of the rock, characteristic of the Beaufort era with its distinctive purple mud, caused by oxides in the water of that period, range from blue to purple blue.

Page 92 An isolated footprint of a small dicynodont named Diictodon, preserved 250 million years ago by the chance deposition of a fine apple green mud in the depression of the then recently made print.

Dark shadow of the valley [indigo]

Page 94 A bouquet of lichen found in Suurkloof.

Pages 96 & 97 The Melk river illuminated by the sun as it flows in a myriad of rivulets across an expanse of flat rock.

PPages 98 & 99

Lying in a certain area of the plain are humps of fossil-bearing mudstone, a cemetery of bones from the Beaufort era, with scatterings of contrasting dolerite pebbles and gravel, residue from a sill. Not far from here lies the tomb of men who once fought bitterly, skirmishing on horseback, all dying in ambush for their cause. / A sense of scale becomes apparent in contrasting light when the massive Rooiberg range is in shadow and the vast plain bathed in light.

Pages 100 & 101

The setting sun illuminates droplets formed at the point where grasses emerge from the shallow water of an overflowing dam. / Shale, verging on silt, fractures in the process of erosion.

Page 102

Elephant feed on succulent bushes amongst trees of Sweet thorn.

cause for wonder

Page 105

The sun rises over the Rooiberg.

Returning red

Page 106

A galaxy of starry lichen clusters brightly on a dolerite boulder in Suurkloof.

Pages 108 & 109

Blood red lichen dapples a boulder. / Fronds of red weed stream out in the current of the Melk's deeper waters.

Pages 110 & 111

Reflected in Petersburg Dam, Siaskop casts its massive shadow across the valley onto the Rooiberg in the east at sunset.

orientation

Page 113

The valley viewed from the south-west looking north-eastwards towards the entrance to Suurkloof and Glenhaven.

Pages 114 & 115

A panoramic view of the valley from the Sneeuberg with peaks on the horizon marking the boundary from east to west: Groot-Suurkop (2,003 m.), Skurwekop (1,792 m.), and Siaskop (1,794 m.).

Page 116

A small stone encrusted with lichen holds a reflecting pool of water after heavy rain.

ACKNOWLEDGEMENTS

I would like to thank the present guardians of Nooitgedacht, Marlene and David McCay, for their invitation to visit the farm in 2002 and for their generous hospitality, friendship and encouragement throughout every stage of this project. I thank also farm managers, Kitty and Richard Viljoen, for their kindness in looking after me, and their readiness to accompany me to far-flung reaches of the valley. In addition I wish to acknowledge the dedicated staff who take such good care of the farm.

I thank Dr Billy de Klerk, Curator of Earth Sciences at the Albany Museum in Grahamstown, for explaining the geological history of the valley to me and correcting my notes. I thank Dr Ralph Clark, Research Fellow of the Botanical Department at Rhodes University in Grahamstown, for introducing me to the floral world on the mountain slopes and identifying for me so many of the plants I have photographed on the farm.

The pages of fragmentary text inserted between the groups of photographs were composed using echoes of phrases taken from books read and re-read. I would like to acknowledge the authors of certain quotations located in these pages; it was W.H. Murray who wrote, "Find beauty; be still" which is quoted by Robert Macfarlane in *The Wild Places*; "...the circle of gifts enters the cycle of nature" is from *The Gift* by Lewis Hyde; "...sporadic appearances and disappearances like legends and rumours through history" is from *The English Patient* by Michael Ondaatje and it was Aleksei Leonov, the astronaut, who observed that, "Earth is small, blue and alone".

I would like to acknowledge and thank my friend Leonard Shapiro who has always been ready to help and advise me. Thank you to my friend and associate at Wild Almond Press, Janene Barnard. I thank Jacques Caumont for so much shared with him, for so much learned from him, and for his continuing friendship.

I dedicate this book to the memory of my father, W.H. Gough-Cooper (1907-1975), who first brought me to South Africa so many years ago.

COLLECTORS & SUBSCRIBERS

The publisher and author would like to acknowledge and thank those who have subscribed to this book, including all those who wish to remain anonymous.

Richard B.M. Anderson
Karina and André Brink
Jacques Caumont
Win Chennells
Mandy Conidaris
Rosemary Currie
Rob and Liz Dudley
Ralph Gentner
Pumla Gobodo-Madikezela
Denis Goldberg
Vivien Gough-Cooper
Ian and Annzie Hancock
Olly Hurren
Wendy and Clive Lucas-Bull
David and Marlene McCay
Patrick McCay
Kezia McCay
Paul Murray
Thomas Neurath
Publishing Print Matters (Pty) Ltd
Markus and Monika Raetz
Trent Read
Rhodes University
Marius Stanz
Sarah Ward
The Humbert Family Trust
Julian Bittiner and Stefanie Victor

First published in South Africa in 2011 by
Wild Almond Press, PO Box 53116, Kenilworth 7745,
in association with Publishing Print Matters (Pty) Ltd
PO Box 640, Noordhoek 7979, Western Cape, South Africa
info@printmatters.co.za
www.printmatters.co.za

A CIP catalogue record for this book is available at the National Library of South Africa.

1,125 copies of this book have been published in three Editions:

Collectors' Edition
25 copies numbered 1 to 25, case bound with linen, presented in a Solander box with an original Polymer Photogravure hand-printed at Warren Editions, Cape Town, signed and numbered 1 to 25 by the author.
ISBN: 978-0-9814417-3-3

Subscribers' Edition
100 copies signed and numbered 26 to 125 by the author, case bound with linen in a slipcase.
ISBN: 978-0-9814417-4-0

Standard Edition
1,000 copies case bound with Wibalin.
ISBN: 978-0-9814417-5-7

Book Design: Nicholas Hales,
from a draft by Jennifer Gough-Cooper and Matt Marshall.

Scans from 35 mm negatives: Frank Hoppler at Photohire, Cape Town

Printed in South Africa by Hansa Print (Pty) Ltd and bound by Graphicraft (Pty) Ltd, Cape Town.